L. McKenna

THE PARENT'S
TAO TE CHING

D0027386

p. 43 — Ugenda's
                Yours or Theirs

Page 56 -
Live one's own life too

                Page 59 -

Page 24 - Fear of failing

THE PARENT'S
TAO TE CHING

■

A NEW INTERPRETATION

ANCIENT ADVICE
FOR
MODERN PARENTS

■

BY WILLIAM MARTIN

FOREWORD BY DAN MILLMAN
ILLUSTRATIONS BY HANK TUSINSKI

MARLOWE & COMPANY
NEW YORK

Published by
Marlowe & Company
841 Broadway, 4th Floor
New York, NY 10003

DESIGN BY PAULINE NEUWIRTH, NEUWIRTH & ASSOCIATES, INC.

Library of Congress Cataloging-in-Publication Data
Martin, William
    The parent's Tao te ching / by William Martin.
        p.   cm.
    ISBN 1-56924-662-9
    1. Parenting.   2. Taoism.   3. Lao-tzu.   Tao te
    ching.   I. Title.
HQ755.8.M358   1999
649'.1—dc21   98-54591
                                                         CIP

First printing, February 1999
Manufactured in the United States of America

To my children, John and Lara.
They are the most wondrous of souls.

CONTENTS

■

AN ART WE
LEARN BY DOING

IT'S A RARE THING when someone is able to improve on a classic—-not only improve it but wrap it in ribbons and offer it as a gift to the modern world. It requires a man of rare wisdom, insight, and heart. Bill Martin is such a man. *The Parent's Tao Te Ching* is such a book. Not since the *Tao of Pooh* has Taoist wisdom transmogrified into something so practical, gentle, and good.

Few things in this world are as important as raising children. In every age, every era, every time and place, children are our treasures, our future, our immortality—-the vital link in the chain of humanity. What better form of service? What better charity to whom we might give of our wealth, our hands, and our hearts? Children remind us of who we were and who we may yet become. They are our innocence, our purity, our potential.

"Children have never been very good at listening to what their parents tell them," James Baldwin wrote, "but they never fail to imitate them." We can only teach by example, Bill Martin reminds us. By improving our own actions, and, in the words of Aldous Huxley, "trying to be a little kinder," we raise not only our children, but our children's standards.

As a father of three and grandfather of two, I've come belatedly to a fuller appreciation of parenthood as a path of spiritual growth. It's not for the faint-hearted, and it's not for everyone. Making babies—having children—is a capacity bestowed by biology, but raising them well is an art we learn by doing. "Mature adults don't necessarily create children," the proverb goes, "but children help create mature adults."

The *Tao Te Ching*, with all its universal wisdom, never struck me as a manual on child rearing, but why not? Universal wisdom applies to every domain, maybe even gardening or motorcycle maintenance. But Bill Martin brings some of the inspiration of Kahlil Gibran, and perhaps even Rumi, to create not abstract poetry, but divinely practical prose. A gift to parents everywhere, *The Parent's Tao Te Ching* is filled with reminders of who *we* can become as we artfully help our children, the same way we might gently guide the branches of a tree to grow straight and tall toward the sun.

Another proverb reminds us that children are not vessels to be filled, but candles to be lit. So are parents. So are we all. By listening to the wisdom of the Tao as we raise our children, we raise ourselves and lift our spirits.

— Dan Millman
San Rafael, California
Author of *Way of the Peaceful Warrior*
December 1998

■

THE *TAO TE CHING* WAS written more than twenty-five hundred years ago. Its authorship is shrouded by legend but is attributed to the legendary Chinese sage, Lao Tzu. It is a book of practical advice for leaders and philosophers, attempting to express glimpses of the inexpressible Tao, or "The Way." Legend has it that Lao Tzu wrote the brief sentences with great reluctance, knowing that the moment the characters appeared on paper the essence of the Tao itself would be lost. Yet his work has become the most widely published book in the world next to the Bible. His brief thoughts have formed the foundation for the modern world's understanding of Taoist philosophy and have deeply affected all philosophical systems.

The *Tao Te Ching* was written in a poetic style

using Chinese characters. A single Chinese ideogram may have a complex set of meanings, the shades of which would require paragraphs of English to capture. Yet any English translation must retain the simple, direct, brief impact of the original. The book you have in your hand is not a translation of the Tao Te Ching. It is a rendering of the wisdom of the Tao specifically for modern parents. For those who wish to explore the *Tao Te Ching* itself there are several excellent English translations available.

In presenting the Tao's message for parents, I have taken what I feel is the essence of each chapter of the *Tao Te Ching* and expanded it into a combination of free verse and pointed advice. I have tried to avoid being overly wordy. An excess of words would violate the spirit of Lao Tzu. I have, however, attempted to be wordy enough to be of practical help.

I have been a student of the *Tao Te Ching* for many years. The depth of its insights and the power of its gentle nurture have deeply affected my spiritual, emotional, and even physical journey. It has especially affected my adventure as a parent of two remarkable children. The great themes that permeate the Tao, such as unity; responding without judgment; emulating natural processes; and balancing between doing and being are central to the health of loving parent-child relationships.

In this volume I have generally used the word, "Tao," to refer to the central concept underlying Lao Tzu's work. It may also be translated as, "The Way," or, "The Way of Life." I sometimes find it helpful to think of it as, "The Way Things Naturally Work." By its very nature this mysterious Tao does not lend itself to definition. As Lao Tzu says, "The Tao that can be told is not the eternal Tao." (Chapter 1, *Tao Te Ching*) Some Westerners have linked the Tao with the idea of God. I resist this link in most cases because of the narrow and sectarian images often conjured by the word, "God." It might be helpful to think of the Tao as the Mystery behind all human ideas and definitions of God, a Mystery that refuses to be caught in the net of human words and definitions. On one or two occasions I have used words like God or Divine Life when referring to the Tao. Please understand that in these cases I am using the words in their broadest possible meaning. The God that can be told is not the eternal God.

I am pleased that Hank Tusinski has produced the brush paintings for this book. In keeping with the nature of the Tao, they are ordinary. That is, they are simple renderings of natural subjects. It is this ordinary, simple, natural nature of Taoist painting that makes it accessible to all. As Lao Tzu used as few words as possible, so the Taoist artist uses as few strokes as possible. In the hands of an artist such as Hank Tusinski, the paintings come alive with a power far beyond the simple ink strokes. I hope that our parenting may find the same combination of boldness, grace, and simplicity.

I am deeply grateful to my beloved spouse, Nancy, who has taught me by her spirit and her own love what no words could ever teach me about the dance of life. Gratitude and blessings also to my wonderful children, Lara and John, whose adventures have warmed, wearied, worried, and filled me with great wonder at the mystery of life and love. They are now adults and I am delighted with them both. But then, their stories are their own, not mine.

Blessings to all parents everywhere. Love and grace to all children.

— Bill Martin
Otter Rock, Oregon
November 1998

THE PARENT'S
TAO TE CHING

■

WORDS OF LIFE

You can speak to your children of life,
but your words are not life itself.
You can show them what you see,
but your showing and their seeing
are forever different things.

You cannot speak to them of Divinity Itself.
But you can share with them
the millions of manifestations of this Reality
arrayed before them every moment.
Since these manifestations have their origin
in the Tao,
the visible will reveal the invisible to them.

Don't mistake your desire to talk for their
        readiness to listen.
Far more important are the wordless truths they
        learn from you.
If you take delight in the ordinary wonders of
        life,
they will feel the depth of your pleasure
and learn to experience joy.
If you walk with them in the darkness of life's
        mysteries
you will open the gate to understanding.

They will learn to see in the darkness
and not be afraid.

Go for a slow and mindful walk.
Show them every little thing that catches your
    eye.
Notice every little thing that catches theirs.
Don't look for lessons or seek to teach great
    things.
Just notice.
The lesson will teach itself.

2.

TAKE CARE WITH LABELS

When you teach your children that certain
     things are good,
they are likely to call all different things bad.
If you teach them that certain things are
     beautiful,
they may see all other things as ugly.

Call difficult things, "difficult,"
and easy things, "easy,"
without avoiding one and seeking the other
and your children will learn self-confidence.
Call results, "results,"
without labeling one as success
and another as failure
and your children will learn freedom from fear.
Call birth, "birth,"
and death, "death,"
without seeing one as good
and the other as evil
and your children will be at home with life.

Notice today how your children label things.
"This stinks."
"That's stupid."
Don't correct them.
Just notice and consider how they learned.
Start today to teach a different lesson.

3.

HAPPINESS IS CONTAGIOUS

If you always compare your children's abilities
to those of great athletes, entertainers, and
    celebrities,
they will lose their own power.
If you urge them to acquire and achieve,
they will learn to cheat and steal
to meet your expectations.

Encourage your children's deepest joys,
not their superficial desires.
Praise their patience,
not their ambition.
Do not value the distractions and diversions
that masquerade as success.
They will learn to hear their own voice
instead of the noise of the crowd.

If you teach them to achieve
they will never be content.
If you teach them contentment,
they will naturally achieve everything.

We all want our children to be happy.
Somehow, some way today
show them something that makes you happy,
something you truly enjoy.
Your own happiness is contagious.
They learn the art from you.

4.

INFINITE POSSIBILITIES

You do not know the true origin of your children.
You call them yours
but they belong to a greater Mystery.
You do not know the name of this Mystery,
but it is the true Mother and Father of your
    children.

At birth your children are filled with possibilities.
It is not your job to limit these possibilities.
Do not say, "This and that are possible for you.
These other things are not."
They will discover on their own what is and is not
    possible.
It is your job to help them stay open
to the marvelous mysteries of life.

It may be interesting to ask,
"What limitations have I, unthinking,
taken upon myself?"
It is very difficult for your child's horizons
to be greater than your own.
Do something today that pushes
against your own preconceptions.
Then take your child's hand
and gently encourage her to do the same.

5.

SEEING TO THE HEART

Some behavior in your children will seem "good"
    to you.
Other behavior will seem unequivocally "bad."
Notice both in your children
without being overly impressed by one
nor overly dismayed by the other.
In doing so you will be imitating the Tao
which sees our behavior as a mask
and sees immediately beneath it
to the good within our heart.

Above all, do not attack your child's behavior
and attempt to change it
by endless talking and scolding.
Stay at your center and look beneath the behavior
to the heart of the child.
There you will find only good.
When you see the heart
you will know what to do.

Of course some behavior is dangerous to the child
and to others.
Express your concern with the behavior.
Do not attack the child.
Consider now a particular behavior that concerns
you.
Meditate carefully and see through
to the heart of your child.
What does it tell you?

6.

RELAX YOUR GRIP

The Tao is continually giving birth
to your children
and to you.
You are not their source.
The Tao is the Great Mother
and the Source of all that is.
Her resources are inexhaustible.

If you empty yourself
of your own expectations,
you will see that your children
will never be
outside Her love.

Your parental responsibilities seem overwhelming
and beyond all reasonable expectation.
You must keep them in school, off drugs and out of
    trouble.
You must get them into college, through college
    and home on time.
You will never have a moment's peace
for no matter how well you and they have done
    until now,
something could always go wrong.
Consider your current concerns.
If God has spaciousness enough
to encompass any difficulty they may have,
can you not relax your grip a bit?

7.

PRESENT FOR ALL

How is the Tao able to be present for all beings?
Because it has no desires for itself
and can therefore accept you
however you may struggle,
however you may fail.
There is always room for you.

Detach yourself from the seeming
successes and failures of your children.
By doing so you become able
to be one with them at all times.
You do not live your life
through your children.
Therefore they are free
to find their own true fulfillment.

Can you encourage your children
without attaching too much importance to the out-
come?
Can you attend your child's game or contest
and cheer for every good play
and every good effort
of all players on both sides?
Can you encourage anyone, on either side, who
makes a mistake?
Does this seem unnatural? Impossible?
Try it.
You will thoroughly enjoy the game
and teach your child a wonderful truth.

8.

MODEL CONTENTMENT

To be a wise parent you must become like water.
It is content to nourish all it touches
without discrimination.
While people struggle to move up,
water flows joyfully down,
filling the low places.

As you care for your children
keep their environment uncluttered,
free of useless gadgets and distractions.
Keep your conversation honest and straight-
        forward,
free of control and manipulation.
Keep your decisions fair and generous,
free of punishment and shame.

As you conduct your life,
be serene and joyful,
content and at peace.
This will be your greatest legacy.

Nothing nurtures a child like a parent
who takes great pleasure from a simple activity,
and is content with the present moment.
Are you modeling contentment
or always wanting "more?"

9.

CAN YOU MAKE ROOM?

If you fill every waking moment
of your children's lives
they will have no room
to be themselves.
If you push them constantly
they will break.
If you burden them with an abundance
of material toys
their hearts will contract in possessiveness.
If you always try to please them
you will be their prisoner,
not their parent.

Don't strive or strain.
Do your work, then rest.
Your children will learn serenity.

Are your children "problems to be solved,"
or people to be loved?
Consider current problems with your children.
Can you create a space,
free from your own anxieties,
in which they are able to find their own way,
feeling your love,
but not your expectations?

10.

AS THEY ARE

When you are with your children
be one with them.
Let every part of your body relax
and become as supple as your child's.
Allow all expectations and anxieties to melt away
so that you can see clearly.
Love them as they are
in this very moment,
without needing to change a thing.

When their lives are filled with trouble
allow events to unfold
without pushing or straining,
and you will understand clearly
what your role should be.

You nourish them without possessing them.
You guide them without controlling them.
You help them without worrying.

Being with your children can be like meditating.
When you are with your child next,
forget the past,
forget the future,
and let your mind and heart come
to be where your body is.

11.

THE STILL POINT

A wheel spins in a circle.
The still point at the center
gives it direction.
Be still.
And your children will see
the way ahead.

A pot has beautiful sides.
The emptiness inside
makes it useful.
Empty yourself of agenda
and you will be available
for your children.

A good house has strong walls.
The space within the walls
makes it a home.
Create space within your heart
and your children
will always rest secure.

Suggesting, guiding, teaching and lecturing,
although well intentioned,
often creates confusion rather than clarity.
Are you filling the air with good advice
and helpful strategies
when you should be still, empty, and spacious?

12.

A QUIET PLACE

Constant stimulation
of your children's senses
creates insensitivity.
They see so much they become blind.
They hear so much they become deaf.
They taste so much they become nauseated.
They desire so much they become forever
unsatisfied.

They do not come to know
that which truly satisfies.

It will be hard to create a quiet place
where your children can find their souls.
You must first quiet your own world
and then approach theirs.
They are accustomed
to the barrage of noise
and will complain loudly in its absence.
But you can find a quiet way.
What can you do today?
A walk?
A book?
A simple game?

13.

FEAR OF FAILURE

Beware of teaching your children
to climb the ladder of success.

Ladders lead down
as well as up.

If you overly protect your children
they will fear failure
and avoid pain.
But failure and pain
are twin teachers
of important lessons.
Unless your children fully experience both
how will they know
they have nothing to fear?

Your children do not learn from their successes.
They learn from their failures.
They must have complete permission to try
and fail,
and discover that they are still OK.
What has your child failed at recently?
How did they react?
How did that make you feel?
How can you each learn from this?

14.

THEIR MYSTERIOUS ORIGIN

Did your children really begin
with the union of your bodies?
Or is their origin more mysterious?

Eternal
means no time,
no beginning,
no end.
Do your children,
who visit you in time,
really reside in eternity?

If you try to grasp them,
they slip away.
They are more than what you see and hear and
        feel.
They belong somewhere else
and only visit here.
So why do you worry?

If the Tao is good, it is completely good
and your children are safe regardless of appearances.
I believed that when my son was struggling with
problems.
I believe it now when he is a handsome, content
adult.
I will believe it if future trouble visits his life.
I believe it.

15.

BE ALERT AND MINDFUL

If you would be a wise parent
be careful in all you do and say.
Know that each action,
each word
has its effect.
Be alert and mindful,
living fully in each present moment.
Treat your children with courtesy
as you would treat a guest.
Be ready in a moment
to let go of one plan
and embark on another
if your inner voice so urges.
Have room within your heart
to hear the voice of both
your children
and your own spirit.
Do not expect fulfillment
from events or people
outside yourself.
Welcome and accept
things as they are.
Welcome and accept
children as they are.

Treat yourself with gentle care.
These qualities emerge naturally,
not by force of will.

16.

EMPTY YOURSELF
OF WORRIES

To survive as a parent
you must empty yourself
of your constant thinking,
planning, and worrying.

You and your children
were born in the Tao,
live in the Tao,
and will return to that same Tao.
If you don't realize this,
you will mistake the sorrow you see in life
for the final word,
and you will become hardened with fear.

But, knowing how things really are,
you gain true confidence.
Being confident,
your mind opens to see your children
as they really are.
Seeing them as they really are,
your heart fills with genuine love for them.
Truly loving them,
you realize your own divine nature.
Realizing your true nature,
you enter eternal life.

These truths lie behind all religious traditions.
Believe them.

17.

NO NEED FOR THREATS

You can control your children
through threats and punishments
and they will learn to fear.
You can control their behavior
by praise and reward
and they will learn to look outside themselves
for approval and for worth.
You can watch over their every movement,
every action, every decision,
making sure they do it "right,"
and they will learn to always
doubt themselves.
Or you can love and guide
without controlling or interfering
and they will learn to trust themselves.

If your child fails at something
merely express your confidence
in their ability to handle the consequences.
If they behave irresponsibly,
merely point out the consequences to themselves
        and others,
and again express your trust that they will learn.
As soon as possible give them another opportunity
to be appropriately responsible.
Do not slip into the downward spiral
of blame,
shame,
and control.
It doesn't work.

18.

NATURAL VIRTUES

All young children naturally love God.
As they grow they are trained by others
and turn instead to piety and religion.

All young children are naturally
at ease with their bodies.
As they grow, they are shamed by others
and become self-conscious and filled with tension.

All young children naturally relate
to other people well.
As they grow they see conflict
and become fearful and guarded.

All virtues arise naturally
until fear and training interfere.
Then virtues disappear
and rules take their place.

Look for the natural virtues of your children.
You may have to pay careful attention.
We are trained not to notice them,
or to distrust them.
But they are the real thing.
They don't have to be taught,
only nurtured.
What natural virtues can you notice in your child
today?

19.

RECOGNIZE
THE INNER REALITIES

If you try to make your children good,
you will make them,
and yourself,
miserable.
Instead show them you believe in
their natural goodness
and all will be blessed.

If you try to make them honor you
you will create instead
resentment and dishonesty.
Instead honor yourself and them
and all will be happy.

If you try to make them successful
you will perpetuate their misery
of endless desires.
Instead enjoy the simple life
and all will find contentment.

You do not have to teach the outward niceties.
You have to recognize the inward realities.
You do not have to make things turn out well.
You have to recognize that all is well.

20.

BE A MODEL OF HONESTY

If you want to become a wise parent
you must be prepared to appear foolish.
You must be willing to say,
"Why should I chase this way and that,
always grasping,
always running?
Nuts!"
Unless you stop following the crowd,
how can your children be free?

To teach your children strength
you must be willing to appear weak.
You must renounce ambition and struggle
and embrace serenity and peace.
You must confess your faults
and embrace your failures.
You must face yourself with honesty
and find the truth of your nature.

Your children need a model of honesty.
If you pretend you have no weaknesses,
and cover them under masks and facades,
your children will learn to do the same
and the game will go on.
Begin today to see,
and accept,
the real you beneath the role.

21.

THE HIDDEN MYSTERY
OF THEIR BEING

Although you give your children names,
their reality is nameless and mysterious.
Their mystery is hidden,
yet plain to see.
It disappears when you stare at it.
It hides when you seek it.
To find it you must look into yourself.
If you can discover the secret of your own life,
you will glimpse the mystery of your children.

Though this mystery cannot be described,
it can be trusted.
You can trust it in yourself.
You can trust it in your children.
How do I know this?
I see it everywhere.

Imagine yourself as a child.
There was someone present there
your parents never knew,
a mystery they could not fathom.
Look at your children closely.
You will never know the mystery of their being.
Can you love them still?

22.

YOUR GREATEST LEGACY

If you want your children to succeed,
show them how to fail.
If you want them to be happy,
show them how to be sad.
If you want them to be healthy,
show them how to be sick.
If you want them to have much,
show them how to enjoy little.
Parents who hide failure, deny loss,
and berate themselves for weakness,
have nothing to teach their children.
But parents who reveal themselves,
in all of their humanness,
become heroes.
For children look to these parents
and learn to love themselves.

Parenting need not be a burden,
one more thing you have to do
and don't do well enough.
Instead consider your failures,
your sorrows,
your illnesses,
and your difficulties
as your primary teaching opportunities.

23.

No Mixed Messages

Natural parents do not give mixed messages.
When they are angry, their children see their anger
and learn it is not to be feared.
When they are sad, their children see their sadness
and learn it can be borne.
When the difficult feelings pass there is no residue.
Their relationship with their children remains
pure and uncontaminated.

It is terribly difficult to parent naturally.
We have learned to repress,
modify, and distrust
our natural responses
until we can barely recognize them.
Of course you should not "dump"
your repressed feelings upon your children.
But you can begin to feel them yourself
and become a friend of your own nature.

This will enable you to express yourself,
appropriately and mindfully, to your children.
There will be less and less hidden agenda
and the fresh air will cleanse everyone.

24.

AGENDAS—YOURS
OR THEIRS?

If you push your children,
they will lose their balance.
If you are always running them here and there,
they will get nowhere.
If you put them in the spotlight,
they will be unable to see their own light.
If you seek to impose upon them
your own ideas of who they should be,
they will become nothing.

If you want them to thrive,
do what you can for their safety,
then let go.

Do you have agendas for your children
that are more important than the children
      themselves?
Lost in the shuffle of uniforms,
practices,
games,
recitals,
and performances
can be the creative and joyful soul of your child.
Watch and listen carefully.

Do they have time to daydream?
From their dreams will emerge
the practices and activities
that will make self-discipline
as natural as breathing.
Encourage these.

25.

CLOUDS OF LIGHT

They look so small and frail
but they are so great and magnificent.
They are born of the same womb
that birthed the cosmos
and knitted together the galaxies.

If you could see them as they truly are,
you would be astounded.
You would see not little children,
but dancing clouds of light,
energy in motion,
swimming in an ocean of love.

They are so much more
than what you see.
As are you.

Life can seem mundane.
But it is not.
Children can seem ordinary,
and troublesome,
and fragile.
But they are not.
You may feel alone,
and separated,
and powerless.
But you are not.

26.

BECOME THE STUDENT

Children are fascinated by the ordinary
and can spend timeless moments
watching sunlight play with dust.
Their restlessness they learn from you.
It is you who are thinking of there
when you are here.
It is you who thinks of then
instead of now.
Stop.
Let your children become the teachers,
and you become the student.

Your children may frequently change the focus
of their attention.
But this is not restlessness.
It is curiosity.
When they are doing something
they are doing only that
until they move on to the next thing.
Watch them.
Let them set the pace.
See what you can learn.

27.

FAN THE SPARK

Your children plan their own education,
like it or not.
You must learn to cooperate with that plan.
If they are drawing,
they become artists.
If they are reading,
they become students.
If they are investigating something,
they become scientists.
If they are helping prepare a meal,
they become chefs.
Whatever they are doing,
they are learning.
And it is, for them,
pure joy.

Can you refrain from judging their interests?
Can you give them room to explore?
Schools do not often do this.
You may be the only one
who can fan the spark of their creativity
into a flame of joy.

28.

TRANSFORMING THE WORLD

The world insists on achievement and progress
and it is full of enmity and strife.
Can you see all this and still help your children
maintain their trust and hope and peace?

Can you accept the world as it is,
yet live according to a different standard?
Can you let your children see
a way of living
that transforms,
heals,
nurtures,
and loves?

If you complain about politics,
and gripe about taxes,
and stew about the sorry state of things
your children will learn to whine instead of laugh.
If you can see in every moment
a chance to live,
and to accept,
and to appreciate,
your children will transform the world.

29.

THE VERY ENERGY
OF THE UNIVERSE

Your children are not mere lumps of clay
waiting for your expert hands.
They are the very energy of the universe
and will become what they will become.
They are sacred beings.
If you tamper with them
you will make everyone miserable.

They will find success,
and failure.
They will be happy,
and sad.
They will delight you,
and disappoint you.
They will be safe,
and at great risk.
They will live,
and they will die.

Stay at the center of your own soul.
There is nothing else you can do.

My son almost lost his life as a teenager.
There was nothing I could do.
I remember accepting that he might die.
I cried for hours.
I got up and returned to my life and to my loves.
Years later, he is a happy, strong, wonderful young
      man—
all because of his choices,
not mine.

30.

GOOD BEHAVIOR

There are many ways to get children
to behave as you wish.
You can force, plead, and bribe.
You can manipulate, trick, and persuade.
You can use shame, guilt, and reason.
These will all rebound upon you.
You will be in constant conflict.

Attend instead to your own actions.
Develop contentment within yourself.
Find peace and love in all you do.
This will keep you busy enough.
There is no need to control others.

If you are able to release even some small part
of your persistent need to control,
you will discover an amazing paradox.
The things you attempted to force
now begin to occur naturally.
People around you begin to change.
Your children find appropriate behavior
emerging from within themselves
and are delighted.
Laughter returns to all.

31.

YOUR CHILDREN ARE NOT YOUR ENEMIES

Your children are not your enemies.
You need not fear them.
Differences with them are not battles
that you must win or lose.
If you lock yourself into seeming warfare,
all perspective becomes lost.
Terrible and hurtful things are said.
The whole family suffers
and the wounds are slow to heal.
Win and lose
are words a family does not need.

You do not have to battle for your authority.
Authority is something you have within yourself.
If your children do not see it,
that is a sorrow,
but you cannot force their seeing.
If you keep this in mind,
many of your battles will disappear.
Difficult times may remain,
but weapons of mass destruction
are no longer needed.

32.

RULES DO NOT GIVE LIFE

Rules do not give life.
The Tao gives life.
And the Tao is seen in butterflies
and in galaxies.
If children were trusted to discover God
in the center of their own hearts
the world would be at peace.

But we have made systems of rules
and institutions of control.
Accept this as the way things are
but always recognize the limitations of rules,
and the dangers of institutions.
Rules can guide a child but cannot define that
      child.
Institutions can nurture a child
but cannot bring that child to maturity.

For a short while,
when your children are young,
you may be able to coerce good behavior.
But goodness of the heart
can never be coerced.
It can only be encouraged

or discouraged.
Consider your family's rules,
spoken and unspoken.
Who made them?
Who benefits from them, and how?
Do they encourage
or discourage your children?

33.

THERE ARE FEW THINGS
YOU MUST KNOW

There are few things you must know
to become a wise parent.
You must know that you are going to die,
for then you will be able to truly live.

You must know when you have enough,
for then you will be content.
You must know how to laugh,
for then you will find healing.

There are many things you need not know.
You need not know everything your children think
        or do.
You need not know their secret dreams and hopes.
You need not know how life will unfold for them,
or for yourself.

Live your own life,
with all your heart,
with all your mind,
and with all your soul.
There is no need to live theirs.
They will do that wonderfully
by themselves.

34.

BE AS THE TAO

In many ways the good parent
must be like the Tao.
But not in ways that you might think.
The Tao loves all of creation,
but does not seek to control.
The Tao nourishes all life everywhere,
but does not judge that life.
The Tao cherishes every person,
but does not grasp or cling.

Can you love without control?
Can you nourish without judgment?
Can you cherish without grasping?
Of course you can,
for the Tao flows through you.

Despite what you may have heard,
God does not
control,
judge,
or grasp.
All of your "God" words
will not teach your children as much
as will your nurture,
and your love,
and your cherishing.

35.

MAKE THE ORDINARY
COME ALIVE

Do not ask your children
to strive for extraordinary lives.
Such striving may seem admirable,
but it is a way of foolishness.
Help them instead to find the wonder
and the marvel of an ordinary life.
Show them the joy of tasting
tomatoes, apples and pears.
Show them how to cry
when pets and people die.
Show them the infinite pleasure
in the touch of a hand.
And make the ordinary come alive for them.
The extraordinary will take care of itself.

You will have to constantly contend
with the pressure for ever more,
and ever bigger,
that culture seeks to impose
on your children
and you.
It takes courage and discipline
to go slow,
live simply,
and see clearly.
But the rewards are great.
What ordinary thing can you do together today?

36.

OPPOSITES ARE NECESSARY

If you want your children to be generous,
you must first allow them to be selfish.
If you want them to be disciplined,
you must first allow them to be spontaneous.
If you want them to be hard-working,
You must first allow them to be lazy.
This is a subtle distinction,
and hard to explain to those who criticize you.

A quality cannot be fully learned
without understanding its opposite.

All your friends,
(especially the grandparents)
will tell you this is nonsense.
But look carefully inside of yourself.
Only the child with a strong sense of self
can be truly generous.
Only the child who discovers his or her bliss
will truly work hard.
Most of what passes as discipline and hard work
is an overlay of coerced behavior.
It has no authentic power or joy.
Only the lazy, undisciplined dreamer
can discover within the source of true discipline
that will bring great success.

37

ENCOURAGE
NATURAL DESIRES

Don't be misled.
God has no desires.
How could that which contains All,
want for anything else?
Yet all true desires
have their fulfillment in God.

Your children will face natural,
and unnatural
desires.
All natural desires
are naturally fulfilled.
Those who chase unnatural desires
will never find rest.
If you can help your children distinguish
between these two,
they will live contented, happy lives.

We all naturally desire to love and be loved,
to belong, to dance and sing,
to find and to live our bliss.
Show your children that these desires
will find their satisfaction
in the natural unfolding of things.

This is a difficult task
for those of us who have been trained
to support the economy
by remaining continuously unsatisfied.
Our children hear far more advertising hours
each and every week,
than they hear our own voice in a month.
Can you show them by your own actions
how true happiness can be found
in loving, living, and dancing?

38.

NO NEED FOR FORCE

Strong parents have no need
to bully and coerce their children.
Weak parents push and shove,
yell and hit,
and still have no power at all.

If good behavior is demanded of children,
without a reservoir of goodness for supply,
nothing is gained.
If religion is preached to children
as external forms
and dogmatic beliefs,
emptiness results.

Wise parents know
that deep within their children
is a free spirit and a goodness
that need not be forced,
only watered
and encouraged.

Don't be deceived
when your children's behavior
seems bad and immoral.
This is not their true nature.
You will not change them
by the force of your will.
Force on your part
will only cloud the issue.
If you were to let go of expectations,
and let yourself be at peace,
what would your children see?

39.

ARE YOU IN THE WAY?

Wise parents let things unfold
with as little interference as possible.
They remain out of the way,
not calling attention to themselves.
Their children discover
the natural harmony of things,
and work out their conflicts
in ways that establish true peace.

When parents interfere,
and constantly meddle in their children's lives,
the natural order is forgotten.
Conflicts are escalated,
learning is curtailed,
and confusion reigns.

There are certainly times when we should guide.
We naturally want to protect our children,
and teach them what we have learned.
But it is best when we let that guidance
be as unobtrusive,
and gentle as possible.
Forcing lessons on our children
may get the immediate results we want.
But our children may be left without discernment,
unable to build internal strength of character.
What are your children in the midst of learning
          now?
Are you in the way?

40.

QUIET THE MIND

Our bodies produce
the bodies of our children.
Our noisy minds produce
the fears of our children.
But the Tao produces
the spirit of our children.

Still the body.
Quiet the mind.
Discover the spirit.

Meditation is not complicated
nor esoteric.
It is a natural skill,
practiced in many variations.
Breathe in and think, "Be . . ."
Breathe out and think, ". . .still."
Once you learn,
teach your children.
You don't have to call it meditation.
Call it, "being still like a mountain."
Bring forth their natural ability
to remain quiet and at rest.
(Yes, they can,
even if for brief periods.
Can you?)

41.

FINDING BALANCE

There are so many paradoxes in parenting
that it is difficult to find balance.
Some don't even try.
They just plunge ahead
ignoring the subtle whispers of wisdom.
Others try half-heartedly,
but resort to old methods
when they get confused.
But some hear wisdom's quiet voice
and make it their own.

They find strength in softness,
power in flexibility,
perfection in mistakes,
success in failure,
clarity in confusion,
and love in letting go.

Parenting paradoxes abound.

Don't let appearances deceive you.

Things may not be at all as they seem.

What's going on with your children right now?

Are you sure?

Or are you just making assumptions?

Buried in the most difficult of times

are polished gems.

Lurking beneath serene surfaces

lie turbulent waters.

Stay balanced.

42.

BEFRIEND SOLITUDE

Learning to handle the many moods
and activities of life
requires solitude.

Do not let the demands
of an overly active world
rob your children of their peace.
Constant stimulation
without the balance of quietness
creates chaos.
The child who early befriends solitude
becomes one with all that is
and inherits everything.

First you must embrace solitude in your own life.
It is more difficult than you think.
Distractions are everywhere.
Even the mind is noisy.
Give your children time to play without agenda,
to read without purpose,
to daydream without limits,
and to discover without fear.
Allow yourself the same.

43.

DOING NOTHING

Doing nothing while your child fails
requires great courage
and is the way of wisdom.
Gentleness when your child misbehaves
requires great self-control
and is the way of power.

Do not succumb to
berating,
scolding,
interfering,
interrupting,
lecturing,
or controlling
your child.
Let your gentle presence
teach all that is necessary.

My father tried to teach me responsibility
by scrutinizing my every action
to make sure it was done right.
I didn't really learn responsibility
until I discovered the consequences
of doing it wrong.
Every mistake your child makes
is another step forward
on the long road to wholeness.
Every time you interfere
you both step backwards.

44.

FIND YOUR OWN MEANING

If you look to your children
to provide meaning for your life,
your life will be meaningless.
If you need them to be successful
to feel successful yourself,
you will always fail.

Your children were not born
to complete your life.
They were born to complete their own.
When you look inside and discover
that you have everything you need,
you will find your freedom.

As long as you perceive
that your life lacks something
you are in danger
of using your children
to satisfy that lack.
This is far too great a burden
for them to bear.
Are you looking to them
when you need to be looking
to yourself?

45.

PERFECTION

If you expect to have perfect children
you will be constantly disappointed
and your children
constantly frustrated.
If you realize that your children
are perfectly themselves
in every moment,
you and your children
will be at peace.

Step back and watch.
You will see that Life
naturally perfects Itself.

Your child's behavior may displease you.
It may even be destructive.
But it is what it is.
It is up to you to understand it
and to use it for good
for your child
and for you.

46.

EACH DAY IS A DANCE

When parents step outside the Way,
they begin to feel vulnerable.
They become afraid of,
and afraid for,
their children.

They lie awake at night,
afraid to confront,
to correct,
to love,
or to hold their children.
Each day they prepare for battle.

But when parents remain in the Way,
they face each day as a dance.
They have nothing to fear,
therefore they produce joy.

I remember many nights of worry.
I remember many days
of tiptoeing around issues,
not wanting to have a confrontation,
hoping I could avoid unpleasantness.
At times I even felt
these lovely persons
were my enemies,
hindering me
and making my life unhappy.
How foolish I was.
There was nothing to fear.

47.

PROVIDING FOR

Your children will make many demands
upon your time and energy.
"Do this for us.
Buy this for us."
They believe that these things
are what they want from you.
And you may begin
to believe it too.

But what they really want
is your innermost heart,
given in vulnerable, honest love.
This is not given
by doing or buying.
The more you do,
the less gets done.
The more you buy,
the less you have.
But if you reveal
your true nature,
you provide them everything.

Of course there are times,
when I do for my children.
It is often my great pleasure.
But the things remembered,
the treasured moments
of sacred time,
have occurred
in the quiet
of gentle conversation,
and honest sharing.

48.

LESS IS MORE

Your children do not need more.
Each day adds more facts,
more gadgets,
more activities,
more desires,
and more confusion
to their lives.

Your task is to subtract.
Each day seek to remove,
to clarify,
to simplify.
Society's wisdom adds,
and confusion grows.
The wisdom of the Tao subtracts,
and serenity flourishes.

If each day one minute less
was spent doing something.
And one minute more
was spent being present,
in simple pleasures,
with your children.
In two months
you would transform your life,
and theirs.
One minute less.

49.

GIVING RESPECT

When your children behave,
give them respect and kindness.
When your children misbehave,
give them respect and kindness.

When they are hateful,
love them.
When they betray your trust,
trust them.

The River of Life nurtures
everything it touches,
without asking for anything.
You will be happy and content
if you do the same.

Believe this difficult truth.
Showing respect in the face of disrespect,
love in the face of hate,
trust in the face of betrayal,
and serenity in the face of turmoil,
will teach your children more
than all the moral lectures
by all the preachers
since the dawn of time.

50.

LETTING GO

If you are always worried
about your children's safety,
you will bind yourself,
and them,
in cords of tension.
If you try to hold them
always close to you,
you will bring yourself,
and them,
only pain.
If you release them
to live their life fully,
and face their death serenely,
your nights will be filled
with restful sleep.

The more I grasped my children
and my own desires for life,
the more dangerous life appeared.
As I gradually let go
plots and plans
and welcomed whatever came,
the safer life became for all of us.

51.

CHILDREN NATURALLY
LOVE LIFE

Your children naturally love life.
Their love of life is spontaneous
and unconscious.
It delights in every nuance of light
and color.
It wonders at every shape
and form.
It dances in their bodies
without self-consciousness.
They are not taught this love.
It cannot be taught,
only lived.

If you live this love for your children
you will guide them,
but never demand a certain response.
You will welcome them,
but never smother them.
You will give birth to them,
but never possess them.
You will nurture their dreams
and guard their self-respect.
They will honor you naturally,
not because of who you are,
but because of who they are.

Don't worry about how your children treat you.
Concentrate on how you treat yourself.
If your children see in you
a sincere celebration of who you are,
they will return eventually
to their natural joy,
in themselves and in you.

52.

ALL IS WELL

All beings belong to the Tao
always.
Sorrow begins
when parents forget this.

Forgetting that you belong,
you cast about for security
and cannot find it.
You look to your children
to bring you meaning,
and they cannot do it.
Seeing your pain,
they forget as well
and everyone is in darkness.

But if you can remember
that all is,
has been,
and will be,
well.
You will bring light to yourself
and to your children.

My father always worried
about the future.
I learned his lesson well.
It has taken me years to unlearn,
and still I forget.
What will your children have to unlearn?
How can you begin now to help them?

53.

DON'T MAKE IT HARDER
THAN IT NEEDS TO BE

Everyone wants to be a wise parent
but few choose this path.
This is unfortunate
for it is an easy path,
filled with joy
and with many rewards.
But it is easy to become sidetracked.
Distractions are everywhere.
As the external pressures mount
be sure to notice what occurs.

Do you pursue career advancement
while your children choose harmful paths?
Do you buy expensive toys
to medicate your feelings
while your children become
lost in the clutter?
Do you sink into depression
while your children hunger for joy?

Don't make parenting harder than it needs to be.
It only requires focus.
Worry is not focus.
Attempting to control is not focus.
Distracting yourself is not focus.
Relaxed, non-fretful, attention
to what is in front of you
right now,
is focus.
What is in front of you right now?
No, not your worries or frets,
what is right here,
right now?

54.

CREATE CLARITY
AND ENCOURAGE FREEDOM

Virtue comes from within your children.
It is a natural part of their being.
It can never be taken from them.
It follows them wherever they travel.
It guides them in all circumstances.
It will cause their life to flourish
and be filled with joy.

Amidst the hundreds of voices
clamoring for their attention saying,
"This way. No, that way,"
your children will learn
to trust their own hearts.
Thus they will act wisely.
You need not worry.

How can you keep from worry?
Look inside yourself.

We don't trust natural goodness.
We think it must be imposed from without.
But all foolish decisions and choices
grow from confusion and fear.
And confusion and fear are amplified
by constant pushing and preaching.
Is there a way you can help
create clarity and encourage freedom?

55.

YOUR CHILDREN HAVE
LESSONS TO TEACH

Your children have important lessons to learn,
but even more important ones to teach.

What can they teach?
How to pay complete attention.
How to play all day without tiring.
How to let one thing go,
and move on to another
with no backward glances.
How to move and sit
with no tension in the muscles,
no stress in the bones.

Thus the wise parent learns,
and grows
younger every day.

How happy would your life become
if every time you taught your children
a new idea or skill from your world,
you stopped and watched until
they taught you one from theirs?
What will you learn from them today?

56.

YOU HAVE
LESSONS TO LEARN

The lessons we most want to teach our children
are the ones we have not yet learned ourselves.
So we continually try to teach
what we do not know.

This is futile.
Try instead to refrain from talking.
Look carefully at the situation.
Listen attentively.
Let your mind be open to new understandings.
You will learn what you need to know.
And you will thus teach your children
how to learn their own lessons.

Nothing teaches children more
than a parent who is willing to learn.
What behavior in your children
makes you anxious?
What does that tell you
about yourself?

57.

REWARD AND PUNISHMENT

Be careful of rules for your children.
Rules diminish responsibility.
Be careful of rewards for your children.
Rewards diminish self-esteem.
Be careful of punishments for your children.
Punishments diminish trust.

Let lessons be imposed
by the nature of things,
not by your own agendas
or your own needs.
Integrity will replace rules.
Contentment will replace striving.
Spirituality will replace religion.
Songs will replace arguments.
Dances will replace battles.

Don't tell me this is overly simple.
Perhaps the most courageous act
of any parent's life
will be that moment
when, even though it breaks your heart,
you stand aside
and let your children
take the natural consequences
of their actions.

58.

You Can Only
Demonstrate

If you carry great expectations
for your children,
they will carry great burdens.
If you try to make them good,
you will create instead their vices.

Let your teaching be subtle.
Let your strength reside
in your flexibility.
Let your virtues be natural
and not affected.

If your children are treated
with modesty,
grace,
forgiveness,
and joy,
what are they likely to learn?

There is nothing more important
than the integrity of your life.
You cannot teach,
impose,
control,
coerce,
or force
any virtue.
You can only demonstrate.
Put your best effort forth
on your own actions,
not those of your children.

59.

BE AMBITIOUS FOR JOY

To experience joy as a parent
you must be free of ambition;
for yourself
and for your children.
Ambition stiffens the muscles
and makes the spirit brittle.
You cannot move with ease
in the winds of change.

But if you release ambition
you can use all of life,
good and bad,
as fuel for the fires of joy.
Because you demand nothing
you have everything,
as do your children.

Do you have ambitions,
hidden or not so hidden,
for yourself or for your children?
Are they reasonable?
What will happen if they are not achieved?
The adolescent years
are filled with discouragement.
Children often compare themselves
to impossible standards
of achievement, beauty, and popularity.
Don't encourage these comparisons.
Encourage joy.

60.

GROWING A GARDEN

Dealing with difficult children
is like watching a garden grow.
Resist the temptation
to pull up the plants
to check on the roots.

In difficult times
children may thrive on conflict.
If you take the bait
the battle rages.
Instead step back,
breathe deeply,
relax,
and stay at your center.
Battles require two parties.
One fighting alone soon tires.

Are there times when,
despite all efforts,
you must impose your will?
Of course.
But remember,
those times are far fewer
than you can imagine.
Is this current battle really necessary?

61.

SELF-ACCEPTANCE

How do children learn
to correct their mistakes?
By watching how you correct yours.
How do children learn
to overcome their failures?
By watching how you overcome yours.
How do children learn
to treat themselves with forgiveness?
By watching you forgive yourself.

Therefore your mistakes,
and your failures
are blessings,
opportunities for the best
in parenting.
And those who point out your mistakes
are not your enemies,
but the most valuable of friends.

Your children will surely notice
the way you handle criticism.
If you get defensive
and launch a counterattack,
they will learn to cover up
and deny their own faults.
Is there something you're covering up now,
with either depression,
self-punishment,
or hostility?
Lighten up.
Accept and forgive yourself
and your children will be blessed.

62.

BE HAPPY

If you have vast wealth,
it will be useless in teaching your children.
If you have great power,
it will be of no avail in securing their happiness.
If you have succeeded admirably in life,
it will not help you keep your children safe.

Remember that you cannot teach
by preaching.
Try to live with peace, contentment,
love and compassion.
This will be your lecture.
This will be your lesson.

The happier I have allowed myself to be,
the happier my children have become.
The more I have become myself,
the more they have done the same.
This has occurred later in my life.
Don't wait.

63.

FACE YOUR PROBLEMS

Face your problems
with your children
while the problems
are still small.
If you give your full attention,
without resentment,
your problems will become
no problem.

A problem is not an interruption
to a serene and happy life.
A problem is an ordinary part
of such a life.
Effort is not required.
If you pay calm attention,
solutions appear naturally.

For years I was afraid
of my children's problems.
I had enough of my own.
I tried to solve their problems
by decree and pronouncement from on high.
So their problems grew and grew.
I was not present to myself.
How could I be present to them?
As I have grown older,
problems are no longer problems,
just life.
They needn't separate us
from our children.
Don't be afraid.

64.

THE ONLY STEP NECESSARY

You do not have to make your children
into wonderful people.
You only have to remind them
that they are wonderful people.
If you do this consistently
from the day they are born
they will believe it easily.

You cannot force your will
upon other human beings.
You can not hurry children
along the road to maturity.
And the only step necessary
on their long journey of life,
is the next small one.

I designed and printed a bumper sticker
when my son was a teenager.
It said,
"My child is an ordinary student,
and a wonderful person."
My son loved it.
Both of my children are,
always have been,
and always will be,
wonderful people.
The same is true of your children.
No matter what.

65.

KNOWLEDGE OR WISDOM?

If you try to teach your children
all the facts and answers
you think they need to know,
they will end up knowing nothing.
If instead you help them look
deep within themselves,
you will have led them to the source,
from where all answers flow.

Don't look to schools
to teach your children wisdom.
Being "Student of the Month"
will not insure happiness.
Your children will have to learn the Way
from other sources,
perhaps from you.

66.

LEAD BY EXAMPLE

If you want your children to follow
along a certain path,
you must lead the way the ocean
leads a river home,
by remaining below it.

If you manipulate, coerce,
and bully your children,
you will have no power at all.
If you lead with humility, gentleness,
and by example,
you will need no power at all.

Power over your children
is the great illusion.
By the time they are six years old,
they will do what they want.
You can bully them
so that they think they want
what you want.
Is that what you want?

67.

COMPASSION, PATIENCE, AND SIMPLICITY

There are only three qualities
you must teach your children.
Compassion, patience, and simplicity.
Some would say this is absurd.
They would teach instead,
ambition, drive, and consumption,
and say it is the way of success.

But if they learn patience,
they see the world as it truly is.
If they learn simplicity,
they see themselves as they truly are.
And if they learn compassion,
they heal themselves
and the world.

Following the Tao as a parent
will often seem opposed
to conventional parenting wisdom.
The confusion lies in ourselves as parents.
We don't know what we truly want,
or who we truly are.
Compassion, patience, and simplicity
cannot be taught
until they are experienced.
And when we experience them,
we lose the need to teach them.
We live them instead.
And then our children learn.

68.

FUN AND GAMES

Before your children learn to win or lose,
they play at games for fun.
But then they come to believe
that they must win
at games,
at business,
and at war.
They even learn to win or lose
at love.

But the Tao teaches
that games are for fun,
that business is for the common good,
that no one wins at war,
and that love endures for all.

Do you play your games for fun?
Do you work for the common good?
Do you divide the world into friends
and enemies?
Do you love selectively?
Can you really "lose" at love?
Examine all of these with honesty.
The answers will reveal
what your children are truly learning.

69.

MARTIAL ARTS

The martial master understands
how to yield and triumph.
When his opponent's blow arrives,
he is not there.
He moves,
yet maintains position,
bends,
but stays balanced.

As a parent you must do the same.
When your children oppose you,
do not meet their opposition with force.
Bend and they will topple.
You will win your point
without harming them.
Thus in yielding,
you will truly triumph.

I wish all parents
could know the art of T'ai Chi Ch'uan.
In this graceful martial art,
balance, softness,
flexibility, and grace
are the means by which
the goal is always reached.
Remember that this does not imply
your children always get their way.
Quite the opposite.
You give them unwavering guidance,
but without violence, tension and grief.
It is a difficult practice,
but filled with great reward.

70.

TRUST THE TAO

The teachings of the parent's Tao
are simple and natural.
Yet when you try to practice them
you will meet with great resistance.
Children have been raised
contrary to the Tao
for countless thousands of years.
No one will support you.

But look around at the effects
of these countless thousands of years.
Then look inside your heart.

The Way of the Tao
has always been here.
Some parents have found it.
Few talk about it.
It seems to them only natural.
They don't call it the Tao.
They just enjoy it.
But for many of us
parenting has been filled with struggle.
There is a better way.
You don't have to learn it.
You already know it.
You only have to trust it.

71.

HAVE CONFIDENCE

The confident parent
is not the one who knows
how to parent in every situation.
The confident parent
is the one who knows
that knowledge will emerge
in the midst of the situation.

This parent's mind
is free of complications,
ready to respond
without preconceptions.
This parent will always act rightly.

My confidence in the future
for my children,
and for me,
exists because I know
we are all part of the Tao.
Come good and bad,
life and death,
that will always be true.
Somehow I will know,
when the time comes,
exactly what to do.

72.

NATURAL SPIRITUALITY

Do not try to teach
religion to your children.
Teach them instead
to marvel at the wonder
of life in all its manifestations.
A natural spirituality will be born
and grow within their hearts.
Trying to teach religion
creates dependence
upon the words of others.
If your children depend
upon their own experience,
they will never go astray.

I served as a clergyman
for two decades of my life.
I know for certain that religion
is as different from natural spirituality
as night is
from the light of day.
Never worry
about your children's souls.
Your child's soul
belongs to the Tao
and is the one reality in life
that is beyond all danger,
always.

73.

OPEN YOUR ARMS WIDE

Wise parents do not strive,
yet their purposes never fail.
They are available,
but never interfere.
They communicate,
but never lecture.
They let their children go,
but never lose them.

These parents are like the Tao.
They open wide their hearts
and hands,
yet never lose a thing.

If I grasp my children
and my other treasures,
I will have only
what my arms can hold.
And even that
slips through my grasp.
But the wider I have opened my arms,
the more and more I find.
If I can ever open wide,
I will have everything.

74.

RIVER OF CHANGE

The child you see today
will not be here tomorrow.
The child arriving home from school,
is different from the one
who left from home this morning.
Every moment is a death
of all that has gone before,
and a birth
of all that is to come.
You must jump into the river
and let it carry you on its journey.
If you try to stop it
you will drown.

Neither we,
nor our children,
will avoid change,
loss, and death.
But our children
will interpret these things
through the vision we give them.
If you can manage
to see through your fear
of these three things,
your children will have
the greatest vision possible.

75.

SPACE AND TIME

If parents are always intruding
into the world of their children,
the children will lose their independent spirit.

If parents impose rule after rule
on the behavior of their children,
the children will lose their self-confidence.

Keep your children safe,
but do not be afraid
to leave them alone.

I once heard a child counselor say,
"You can never spend too much time
with your children."
Yes, you can.
Children need, of course,
the assurance of your presence.
But they also need,
at every age,
plenty of space to play the games,
to imagine the futures,
and to dream the dreams
of childhood.
Too much time spent together
may be serving your needs,
not theirs.

76.

HOLD TIGHT
ONLY TO COMPASSION

It has been said by experts,
"You must be consistent,
or your children will be confused."
Nonsense.
Who among us is consistent?
Circumstances are always changing.

Children become confused
when parents become rigid,
holding rules above love.
Be consistently flexible.
Hold tight only to compassion.

As people age they become
either soft and supple,
or hard and brittle,
both in mind and body.
I have seen profound examples
of each type,
so have you.
Which are you becoming?

Children are flexible
in body and in spirit.
The greatest gift we can give them,
is to become the same.

77.

NEVER SEEK TO TRIUMPH
OVER YOUR CHILDREN

Parents who follow the Tao,
never seek to triumph
over their children.

They have no need of winning
to protect their position.
Their position is secure.
Nor do they let their children
triumph over them.
This would harm their children.

Winning and losing
have no meaning
to such parents.
They always find the balance
between too much
and too little.
No one is afraid of them.
They are afraid of no one.

There are times,
especially when they are young,
that we must impose our will
upon our children.
But do so only for their safety.
It is all too easy
to use our size and power
to intimidate our children
and get our way.
This does not teach the Tao.

78.

DIFFICULTIES ARE
OVERCOME BY YIELDING

Parents facing hardship and sorrow
must become like water.
They must embrace
the hardest things of life
and enfold them with their heart.
Death and loss are overcome
with gentleness and serenity.

We all want to protect our children
from the sorrow and loss of life.
We cannot.
But the way we behave
when faced with these things
will give our children all they need
to remain at peace.
Remember water.
Nothing hard can stop it.
What hardships are you facing?
What are your children learning
as they watch you?

79.

REFUSE TO LEVEL BLAME

Parents of the Tao
refuse to level blame.
They watch the evening news
without complaining.
They observe the failures of others
and never gloat.
When their children
let them down
they remain serene.
They fulfill their own duties
and never worry about others.

There is never a need to blame our children
for anything.
We can, of course, correct them.
We can guide them gently
and with wisdom.
But blaming our children
for their faults
is not the only problem.
Monitor your conversations
for a seven day period.
Make a note each time
that you complain or blame

concerning anything.
Your children listen.
Are they learning to blame others,
or to take constructive action?

80.

EMPTY NEST

If parents follow wisdom,
their children remain happy.
They content themselves
with simple pleasures
and don't look to constant stimulation
to keep themselves amused.

They love being at home
and don't have to go elsewhere
for approval and acceptance.
When they leave home
to continue with their own adventure,
they carry with them
confidence, contentment, and joy.
And their parents watch them leave,
with satisfaction, peace, and happiness.

The "empty nest syndrome"
should never bother
parents of the Tao.
Of course we'll miss our children.
But all their lives we have helped them
embrace life and welcome change.
We have learned to do the same.
New moments await us.
Our nest,
and theirs,
is never empty.

81.

WITHIN THE STREAM

Words will never bring
our children to a knowledge of the Tao.

We don't need to argue.
We don't need to teach.
We don't need to push.
We don't need to strive.

We only need to live
content within the Stream.

My words are over.
I wrote them for myself,
that I might hear them often enough
to begin to understand them.
And as I begin to understand them,
may I begin to live them.
If looking over my shoulder
has brought to you some pleasure,
I am content.

William Martin, the father of two grown children, John and Lara, has been a student of the Tao for ten years. A graduate of the University of California, Berkeley, and Western Theological Seminary, he has worked as a research scientist for the Department of the Navy, a clergyman, and a college instructor in counseling, communications, and the humanities. Today he operates, with his wife, Nancy, The Still Point, an educational and consulting center in Chico, California. He conducts workshops and seminars on subjects including tai chi chuan, Zen, stages of spiritual development, meditation, and religious burnout. He and his wife live in Chico, California.

William Martin can be reached by e-mail at parentstao@innocent.com.